READING CHAMPION

Goldilocks met Three Bears

by Damian Harvey and Irina Mileo

W
FRANKLIN WATTS
LONDON•SYDNEY

Mummy Bear, Daddy Bear, and Baby Bear lived in a cottage in the middle of the woods.

One morning, Mummy Bear made porridge for breakfast.

“The porridge is too hot to eat,” said Mummy Bear. “Let’s go for a walk until it cools down.”

Goldilocks was walking through the woods. She saw the bears' cottage and went to look through the window. She could see three bowls of porridge on the table.

“Yum, I love porridge!” said Goldilocks.

So she opened the door and went

into the kitchen.

First, Goldilocks tried Daddy Bear's porridge.

"Yuck!" she cried. "That's too salty!"

Next, she tried Mummy Bear's porridge.

"Yuck!" she cried.

"That's too sweet!"

Then she tried Baby Bear's porridge.

"Yum!" she said. "That's just right!"

And she ate it all up.

Next, Goldilocks went into the living room. She saw three chairs.

First, she tried Daddy Bear's chair.

"That's too hard!" she cried.

Next, she tried Mummy Bear's chair.

"That's too soft!" she cried.

Then, she tried Baby Bear's chair.

"That's better!" she said and sat down.

But Goldilocks was too heavy and the chair broke.

"Oh no!" said Goldilocks.

“I think I will have a look upstairs,” said Goldilocks.

She was about to go up the stairs when she heard a sound.

The three bears were back.

Goldilocks hid.

The bears were looking forward to eating their porridge. They looked in their bowls.

"Someone's been eating my porridge!" growled Daddy Bear.

"Someone's been eating my porridge!" grumbled Mummy Bear.

“Someone’s been eating my porridge,” cried Baby Bear. “And they’ve eaten it all up!”

Goldilocks felt sad. She wished she hadn’t eaten the porridge.

Next, the three bears went into their living room.

“Someone’s been sitting in my chair!” growled Daddy Bear.

“Someone’s been sitting in my chair!” grumbled Mummy Bear.

"Someone's been sitting in my chair!" cried Baby Bear. "And they've broken it!" Goldilocks felt sad. She wished she hadn't broken the chair.

The three bears were just about to go upstairs, but then they saw Goldilocks.

"Who are you?" cried Baby Bear.

“I’m Goldilocks,” said Goldilocks.

“And I’m sorry. It was me that ate your porridge and broke your chair.”

Then she started to cry.

The three bears were sad when they saw Goldilocks cry.

"You could help us make some more porridge," said Mummy Bear.

"And you could help us fix the chair," said Daddy Bear.

"Yes, I will!" said Goldilocks.

Goldilocks liked helping the bears. She went to their house every week, and soon they became best friends.

Story order

Look at these 5 pictures and captions.
Put the pictures in the right order
to retell the story.

1

The bears come back from their walk.

2

Goldilocks feels sad and starts to cry.

3

The bears decide to go out for a walk.

4

Goldilocks and the bears are friends.

5

Baby Bear's porridge has been eaten.

Independent Reading

This series is designed to provide an opportunity for your child to read on their own. These notes are written for you to help your child choose a book and to read it independently.
In school, your child's teacher will often be using reading books which have been banded to support the process of learning to read. Use the book band colour your child is reading in school to help you make a good choice. *Goldilocks Met Three Bears* is a good choice for children reading at Purple Band in their classroom to read independently. The aim of independent reading is to read this book with ease, so that your child enjoys the story and relates it to their own experiences.

About the book

Goldilocks discovers a house in the woods. She doesn't realise that the house belongs to three bears – and she soon wants to make amends for having eaten some of their breakfast and broken a chair. This story offers a different ending to the well-known tale.

Before reading

Help your child to learn how to make good choices by asking: "Why did you choose this book? Why do you think you will enjoy it?" Look at the cover together and ask: "What do you think the story will be about?" Ask your child to think of what they already know about the original version of the story. Then ask your child to read the title aloud. Ask: "Why do you think Goldilocks is giving out porridge to the bears?
Remind your child that they can sound out the letters to make a word if they get stuck. Decide together whether your child will read the story independently or read it aloud to you.

During reading

Remind your child of what they know and what they can do independently. If reading aloud, support your child if they hesitate or ask for help by telling the word. If reading to themselves, remind your child that they can come and ask for your help if stuck.

After reading

Support comprehension by asking your child to tell you about the story. Use the story order puzzle to encourage your child to retell the story in the right sequence, in their own words. The correct sequence can be found on the next page.

Help your child think about the messages in the book that go beyond the story and ask: "Why does Goldilocks cry when she sees the three bears come home? How does she try to make up for her previous actions?"

Give your child a chance to respond to the story: "What was your favourite part and why? What would have happened if Goldilocks had stayed hidden?"

Extending learning

Help your child understand the story structure by using the same sentence patterning and adding different elements. "Let's make up a new story about Goldilocks. She is hungry and finds an underground burrow. What animal family could be living there? What might Goldilocks do? In the classroom, your child's teacher may be teaching different kinds of sentences. There are many examples in this book that you could look at with your child, including statements, commands and questions. Find these together and point out how the end punctuation can help us decide what kind of sentence it is.

Franklin Watts
First published in Great Britain in 2024
by Hodder and Stoughton

Series Editors: Jackie Hamley and Melanie Palmer
Development Editors and Series Advisors: Dr Sue Bodman and Glen Franklin
Series Designers: Cathryn Gilbert and Peter Scoulding

A CIP catalogue record for this book is
available from the British Library.

ISBN 978 1 4451 9082 2 (hbk)
ISBN 978 1 4451 9084 6 (pbk)
ISBN 978 1 4451 9083 9 (ebook)

Printed in China

Franklin Watts
An imprint of
Hachette Children's Group
Part of Hodder and Stoughton
Carmelite House
50 Victoria Embankment
London EC4Y 0DZ

An Hachette UK Company
www.hachette.co.uk

www.reading-champion.co.uk

FSC
www.fsc.org
MIX
Paper | Supporting
responsible forestry
FSC® C104740

Answer to Story order: 3, 1, 5, 2, 4